The Practical Helps Library™

Helping Believers Live In A World With No Normal!

Roger Henri Trepanier

Scripture taken from

This book is available for purchase
in print format or as an eBook
on all major distribution channels

The author may be contacted at the website:

http://www.pilgrimpathwaypublications.com

Trademarks:

This book is dedicated to all those on earth who by the grace, mercy, and love of God have come to believe in God through faith in His precious Son, The Lord Jesus Christ! May the following be true of all such in these last days of the present age:

"Do all things without grumbling or disputing; so that you will prove yourselves to be blameless and innocent, children of God above reproach in the midst of a crooked and perverse generation, among whom you appear as lights in the world, holding fast the word of life…"

Philippians 2:14-16 in part

Titles available from Roger Henri Trepanier in The Truth Seeker's Library™ series:

God Did Not Create Human Beings To Die… But To Live On… Eternally!
Finding Comfort And Encouragement In The Promises Of God In The Last Days
How We Know For Sure That We Are Living In The Last Days!
Have You Ever Wondered What Happens After Death?
An Introduction To The New World That Is Coming On The Earth
Deeper Truths Of The Christian Life
Evangelism As God Intended
Keeping On Serving God In The Last Days
The Mysterious World Of Angels And Demons
No One Loves As He Loves!
Thanks Be To God For His Indescribable Gift!
The Church Is Very Much Alive, Well, And Growing!
Tracing The Steps Of The Son Of God From Eternity To Eternity!
War, And Going To War, Is Simply Not Of God!
God Never Meant Prayer To Be A Mystery!
Health Is One Of God's Great Blessings!
Removing The Mystery Surrounding Baptism!
This World's Return To Paganism Is Almost Complete!
Removing The Mystery Surrounding Heaven!
God's Covenants Were Meant For Mankind's Blessing!
The Four Ages Of Time
The Awesomeness Of God!
A Call To A Biblical Christianity!
Believers! Look Up! Our Homegoing Is Any Day!
Why God Created The Male And The Female!
This Earth Was Never Meant To Be The Believer's Home!
It Is A Terrifying Thing To Fall Into The Hands Of The Living God!
The Rapture Of The Church Is God's Last End Time Event!
This Present Earth Will One Day Be Eternal Hell!

Titles available from Roger Henri Trepanier in The Practical Helps Library™ series:

Learning to Overcome The Perplexities Of This Present Life
So, I Hear You Want To Work With Seniors?
I Will Not Have This Man To Rule Over Me!
Spiritual Truth To Warm The Heart!
Fasten Your Seatbelts: Turbulence Ahead!
Living A Normal Christian Life In An Increasingly Abnormal World!
If You Have Jesus; You Do Not Need Drugs!
To Do God's Will Is To Have A Foretaste Of Heaven!
This World Is Ready For The Rule Of The Antichrist!
President Trump And The Q Movement Versus Satan And The DEEP STATE
More Of God's Great Promises For Comfort And Encouragement!
Alert! The C-Virus Pandemic Was Satan's Practice Run For A New World Order
The Days Are Evil! The Time Is Short! Be Saved From This Perverse Generation!
Your Worldview Determines Your Wellbeing And Eternal Destiny!
What We Are Watching Is The Spirit Of The Antichrist At Work!
A Sure Cure For Loneliness!
Will God Allow President Trump To Regain The White House?
The Antichrist Arises Out Of Europe And Is About To Appear On The World Scene!

Titles available from Roger Henri Trepanier in The Christian Fiction Library™ series:

The Beginning Of A New Dawn
It Is Never Too Late For Love!
The True To Life Musings Of Fred And Ernie
Between A Rock And A Hard Place!
Love Knows No Boundaries!
A Woman Worth Pursuing!

Love Is More Than Just A Four Letter Word!
The Twists And Turns Of The Life Of Faith!

Titles available from Roger Henri Trepanier in The Word Of God Library™ series:

God's First Letter To The Thessalonians
God's Second Letter To The Thessalonians
God's Letter To Believers Through Jude
God's Three Short Letters To Believers Through John
God's Letter To Scattered Believers Through James
God's Letter To Titus
God's Prophetic Word To Mankind Through Daniel
God's Letter To Philemon And God's Letter To The Colossians
God's Consummation Of All In The Book Of Revelation
God's Letter To The Philippians
God's First Letter Through Peter
God's Second Letter Through Peter
Jonah, God's Reluctant Prophet!
God's Letter To The Galatians
God's Providence In The Book Of Esther
God's Love For Gentiles In The Book Of Ruth
God's Letter To The Ephesians
God's First Letter To Timothy
God's Second Letter To Timothy
Jesus' Sermon On The Mount: Matthews 5 to 7
Jesus" Parting Words Of Love To His Own: John 13 To 16
God's Letter To The Romans Through The Apostle Paul
God's Letter To The Hebrews

INTRODUCTION

The world can be divided into two distinct groups at this critical time in world history: Those who are unaware of what is going on in the world, which makes up the majority of humanity; and those who are aware to some varying degree, in terms of not accepting the prevailing narrative on any topic, but willing to apply critical thinking and not being afraid to question things that do not resonate with one's value system. It would be nice to say that all believers are in the second category, but unfortunately that is far from being the case!

This is an important book because it touches on many issues that touch all of our lives, whether believers or unbelievers, and no matter where one might be living on this planet we call earth. These are difficult times, as all can attest to, with this especially being true for those at the bottom half of the socio-economic scale, and especially in the poorest countries of the world. The unfortunate part is that those who need to hear the truth of this book are not likely to be the ones to have an opportunity to read it!

It is hoped that those who do read this book and are believers will be led of God to help those less fortunate that are everywhere around us. For instance, at the start of this so-called 'pandemic' in 2020, after lockdowns were occurring in country after country, I found myself entering the parking lot of one of the grocery stores where I live. At the entrance was a woman with a large sign, which read, "Will clean house in exchange for food." When I went to talk with her, I found out she was a widow with two young sons, and she was trying to make a living by cleaning other people's homes for pay. But since there was a lockdown and people were all home, then that meant that her income was almost nil, and she was already in arrears on her hydro bill, and could not afford to put gas in her car, or even pay her rent. If I had walked away without helping this family in their moment of need, then anyone would have been justified in saying that I was a Christian in name only!

And so, what we will be doing in this book is look at a number of areas that touches all of our daily lives and seek to offer helpful solutions, at times based on God's word, and at times based on my own personal experiences. No matter what the source of the help, we will attempt to always be practical, in terms of helping people 'where the rubber meets the road,' since that is the place we all find ourselves in, no matter what one's position might be at this time in this present life!

We are to also note that there is an Addenda at the back of the book with two sections. In Addendum A, we have a discussion of the nature of man and the consequence of sin; while in Addendum B, we have a presentation of the gospel, which is the good news that God has given in His word regarding His Son, The Lord Jesus Christ, for any reading this book who might not as yet have this vital personal relationship with God through faith in His Son. The greatest tragedy that can befall any human being born into this world is to spend a lifetime here and never come to personally know God, and so never being able to access the peace, the joy, the grace, the love, and the provision that God gives to those who have become part of His family on earth through a new spiritual birth!

What should also be mentioned before closing this Introduction, because we are all somewhat curious by nature, is that after completing 21 years of formal education, and then spending almost 28 years working in Project Engineering and Management in the Corporate offices of two large utilities, God called His servant as a non-denominational evangelist in early 1999, and then sent him out over two thousand miles, away from family and friends, to the place of service God assigned, which is where His servant has been, and is still serving Him, as evangelist, author, and counselor. The author is a widower with three adopted children, all now married with a family of their own.

Please note the two websites listed below, which have been established for the purpose of interacting with readers and for gospel ministry:

http://www.pilgrimpathwaypublications.com

http://servantofmosthigh.com

And now my prayer is that God will richly bless you as you read this book, and greatly minister to every need in your life, as only God can! To Him be all praise, honor, and glory, with thanksgiving, both now and forevermore! Amen.

CONTENTS

“Children, it is the last hour; and just as you heard that ANTICHRIST IS COMING, even now many antichrists have appeared; from this we know that it is the last hour.”

1 John 2:18

“And the great dragon was thrown down, the serpent of old who is called THE DEVIL AND SATAN, WHO DECEIVES THE WHOLE WORLD; he was thrown down to the earth, and his angels were thrown down with him.”

Revelation 12:9

CHAPTER ONE

Why there no longer is any normal anywhere on earth!

As we begin this most important book, we need to grasp the fact that the world that we knew and lived in before the so-called 'pandemic,' which began on March 11, 2020, and which many have dubbed a 'plandemic,' is now forever gone! And please understand that my purpose here is not to discuss the 'pandemic' itself of the last two years, as I have already made my position clear in the book that I have already written and have had published on this subject.

Rather, what needs to be said at this time is that we all need to be aware of what the AGENDA is that is behind all the events that have taken place in the world since March 11, 2020! Those who are believers are no doubt aware that there is an evil fallen angelic being, whom God has called Satan, the devil, who from the beginning of his fall into sin has been leading the human race astray through his deceptions!

For what needs to be grasped here is that from the dawn of the creation of this present earth – and the fall of this angelic being known as Satan, the devil – this evil character has been attempting to not only remove any knowledge of God from this earth, but has in fact been attempting to establish a kingdom to rival God's own on this present earth! In other words, the one goal driving Satan, the devil, is to be RULER OVER ALL CREATION, INSTEAD OF GOD! And in order to achieve that he needs a world that is united in a common purpose – but unfortunately not for good, but for evil – with that common purpose being to have a ONE WORLD GOVERNMENT established on earth, with a one world religion!

The amazing thing is that God has already told us that the devil is going to do this! One only has to read Revelation 13 in the Bible, where God will allow the devil, there seen as the dragon, to rule over this earth through his antichrist, who is the first beast of Revelation 13:1, doing so for a period of seven years, which could start at any moment! In fact, the antichrist's rule will begin as soon as God removes all believers from the earth, as God discloses at 1 Thessalonians 4:14-17), who are now, through The Holy Spirit indwelling each, being used of God to restrain the evil in this world! When the antichrist – as Satan's evil counterfeit to God's Son, The Lord Jesus Christ – comes on the world scene, he will be assisted by the false prophet, who is the second beast mentioned at Revelation 13:11.

And so, as the antichrist rules over the nations of the earth as political leader over a one world government during those coming seven years, the false prophet will be assisting him as religious leader over a worldwide false religious system, with both of these evil characters being under the authority of Satan, the devil!

What is very important to grasp here is that this coming seven year period, in which the antichrist will be ruling over all the nations of the earth, is a set event ON GOD'S CALENDAR! In other words, only God is Almighty, in that only He has the power to carry out His will all the time on earth, and He is also the only Sovereign, meaning that He is at all times in control of every single person, event, circumstance, and situation that ever occurs, so that He is always working in accordance with a plan for the ages of time, all designed for the good of believers and for the ultimate defeat and eternal judgment of all the unbelieving!

And in order for the devil to bring his AGENDA to pass on earth, in terms of bringing in that rule of his antichrist and false prophet, he needs that one world government to be established. You may have heard the term, A NEW WORLD ORDER' before. Well, this term is simply referring to all the unbelievers of the world being used by the devil – knowingly or unknowingly – to work together in order to bring in that one world government so the antichrist can begin his rule over the nations of this earth.

And because we have now reached the point in time when this event IS ABOUT TO OCCUR, then this means that great upheaval has been occurring in all nations on earth since March 11, 2020, where GLOBALISTS worldwide – as those being energized by the devil to bring in that new world order – are working feverishly to bring in the devil's agenda, which consists of at least ten things that can be identified here. These ten things that are at present being outworked are what is causing all the upheaval in the world, and why THERE NO LONGER IS ANY NORMAL for any human being on earth!

And so, those ten things which the devil is working to have occur as soon as possible are as follows:

1) A one world government under a one world political leader

What should be grasped here is that when the devil's antichrist is revealed upon the earth, there will ALREADY BE an established structure for a one world government to take place! We already have the United Nations (UN), with all its various agencies covering every aspect of human life on earth, as one such existing structure!

2) A one world religion under one leader

As we see from Revelation 13:11-18, there is a religious leader coming on the world stage, as the false prophet, who will be over the false religious system of the devil. And so again, any movement on earth – such as the establishment of the World Council of Churches (WCC) in 1948 and continuing on at present – working toward unifying the religions of the world should be seen as not only moving us closer to the end of the present third age, but also leading the world toward the devil-inspired false religious system being brought in as a one world religion!

3) A cashless society, which requires the introduction of a digital currency

This specifically relates to Revelation 13:17 – in the second half of that future seven year period – where we see that the antichrist, through the false prophet, will cause all those on earth, who refuse to give him worship, will not be able to buy or sell. And in order for that to be achieved, it is obvious that the antichrist will need to be able to control every transaction on earth, which can only be achieved if there is no cash, and all payments are digital. This also means that a digital currency and digital methods of payment must be in place, which the antichrist world government will be able to control.

4) A digital identification mark

A digital identification mark (ID) is required as a means to control who buys and sells. This ID will be biometric in nature, that is, will use some part of the human body to identify that it is really you. At Revelation 13:16, God says that this ID will be either on one's right hand or on one's forehead.

5) Control of all forms of media

It is obvious that the world government under the antichrist will be in control of all forms of media, such as television, radio, internet, social media platforms, and all means of communications, so as to be able totally control what people hear, see, read, and therefore think!

6) A surveillance state

It should also be obvious that the world government that the antichrist will rule over will be able to not only identify individuals, but to also know where they are at any given moment of the day or night, including knowing what they are doing. This means that monitoring cameras, facial recognition systems, license plate readers, and drones must be in place the world over to constantly monitor people!

7) Control of population increases

It should also be obvious that the lower the population, the easier it is to control it, which further means that population increases must be minimized by whatever means may be necessary to achieve this, such as birth control methods, forced sterilization, mind control, drugs, eugenics, transhumanism, and according to Bill Gates' 2015 TED talk, even the use of vaccines!

8) A disarmed population

It should also be obvious that a one world government under the antichrist needs a disarmed population, so that people cannot defend themselves, nor rise up against the established authorities. This therefore means that all things that can be used as a weapon must be confiscated and destroyed, including their means of production!

9) Effective means of rounding up and killing off enemies of the state

The antichrist will also have at his disposal efficient means of quickly tracking down, rounding up, and eliminating any person deemed an enemy of the state. There are in existence at present killer robots, drones, and similar means, that can be programmed through artificial intelligence systems to track and kill individuals anywhere in the world.

For instance, one only needs to show a drone, that has been programmed by AI, a picture and an address of a person, and then let the drone track and kill the person with a bullet, an explosive device (if more than one at a time), or a poisonous dart. These means are all currently available!

10) Removal of the United States from being world leader; economically, militarily, and diplomatically

As everyone knows, the United States is at present (or at least was until Joe Biden) the world leader; economically, militarily, and diplomatically. The United States has been since WW1 the elephant in the room, in that it only had to speak or make a move and it affected the rest of the world.

Friends and foes of the United States all knew this! That is why the devil knows that in order to bring in a one world government under the antichrist, he needs to eliminate the United States from being leader of the world, as that is a position that the world government under the antichrist must hold!

It is clear from God's word, and especially the book of Revelation, that this will indeed be the case when the antichrist does come on the world scene, in that the United States will indeed have been removed from being world leader economically, militarily, and diplomatically! And with Joe Biden's so called 'Presidency,' the United States has indeed been rendered, in a very short time, a third world banana republic, as a gift to the evil one!

"If the foundations are destroyed, what can the righteous do?"

Psalm 11:3

CHAPTER TWO

The reality to be grasped is that there never has been a normal on earth!

What needs to be pointed out and grasped in this chapter is that THERE HAS NEVER BEEN A NORMAL ON THIS EARTH! For what we all need to realize is that from the moment that Adam and Eve sinned against God, when tested by God in the garden of Eden, the rule over this earth, which had been given to them by God (noting Genesis 1:26), was transferred to Satan, the devil, which he still has! Let us note what God tells us at 1 John 5:19 in this regard, "We know that we (believers) are of God, and that the whole world (of unbelievers) LIES IN THE POWER OF THE EVIL ONE."

There are TWO REASONS why we as human beings on earth NEVER NOTICED THE EVIL THAT WAS PRESENT in this world. The first reason to be aware of is that this evil has been operating in the shadows, that is, behind the scene, out of public view! Then the second reason is that the time in world history had not arrived yet for the devil to bring in his antichrist on the world scene! As we have seen in the previous chapter, while the devil has had the ambition to rule over this earth instead of mankind under God, yet it was not on God's calendar for him to yet achieve this. What that has meant then is that the nations of the world have been allowed to operate UNDER THE ILLUSION OF THERE BEING A NORMAL, WHEN IN REALITY THERE NEVER WAS ONE!

Let us take three examples that most people alive today would be able to relate to, and only going back to the Second World War. THE ONE EXAMPLE we can make mention here is that during the Second War we saw the devil use Hitler to attempt to set up a one world government under his leadership, with many countries of the world being more than happy to align with him! Then immediately after WW2, as supposedly an attempt to prevent such a dictator from arising again in the future, we saw the setup of the United Nations, which every country on earth was soon more than eager to join. So what the devil was not able to achieve through Hitler, he was now to use the United Nations to move his agenda forward of establishing a one world government on earth, which has worked marvelously for him!

Then a SECOND EXAMPLY that can be given, which is again only from WW2 onward – and this was the case in many countries – the women had to go work in the war armament factories, since the men that could go to war had been enlisted! What this meant, of course, is that after the war a lot of women continued to work outside of the home, which increased even more as time went on, even though now there was no longer any great necessity for them to do so! And as many know, governments worldwide even made it easier than ever for them to work outside the home with all kinds of policies and programs being introduced to facilitate this! One prime example of this being the approval of the birth control pill by most governments around the world!

However, as those who are believers especially would understand, A STABLE HOME is the foundation upon which God intended societies the world over to be built! And of course, the devil also knows this, which is why he has been working in the background through the unbelievers of this world to chip away at this important foundation! And as all would be aware, when the wife started working out, then that has meant all kind of friction and dissension in the home, from the sharing of financial obligations, to the sharing of household duties! And that friction and dissension has more often than naught led to many separations and divorces, which have grieved God, but has delighted the devil!

I have been fortunate to always have my wife be able to stay at home, of her own accord, for she knew that she just had to be there for when the children came home from school, and also to be home to make supper, so that we could all sit down together as a family. I can attest to the countless times that one could hear on weekdays, all over the office, the women who did work talking to their kids, who had just arrived home from school without any parents there, and now these mothers were semi-yelling on the phone, saying things like, "No, you cannot do that," or "no, you cannot go there," or "no, you cannot go ahead and eat that, but only eat this until I get home, or it will spoil your supper!" How the devil was delighted to see all this, although many certainly did not realize that the foundation of stable homes was slowly being chipped away!

A THIRD EXAMPLE that can be mentioned here, which is also since WW2, is the introduction of the TELEVISION! What this now meant was the devil having access to every home that had a television, which before too long was almost every home! In September of 1987, my wife and I were vacationing in Cancun, Mexico, and took a side trip one day to the Yucatan Peninsula to see many of the old ancient Aztec ruins. On the way back, the bus stopped at a village, so that we could all get out and walk around to see how the people lived. Most of the men who lived in that village worked at various construction sites or service establishments in Cancun. In any case, in one hut, with no windows or doors, there was a woman and children sitting down on the ground with a television on a crate sitting in the middle of the room! There was one wire running from the electricity pole at the road, which powered the TV and lit the one light bulb!

What the introduction of the television into every home has done is to give outside forces the ability to control what every family was to watch on that TV set! My earliest recollections were wresting out of Madison Square Garden in New York, and Roy Rogers and Tonto! Seems harmless enough, but unfortunately that foreign object soon became the focal point of every home, in terms of what people now turned to for everything from the news, sports, current events, documentaries, and yes, let us not forget the movies!

What this has meant then is that everyone was being programmed to accept a common narrative that all the major networks, such as ABC, CBS, and NBC, were themselves holding, which meant leading people to hold similar views on the major issues, which of course meant it easier to control people in living a certain lifestyle and buying certain products! It is important to keep in mind that what is not directly of God in this world has an evil agenda behind it, even though on the surface, everything appears to be good and wholesome!

What made it easy for the devil to advance his evil agenda century by century is that each generation that is born into this world thinks that what they are born into is NORMAL! A child growing up at a certain point in time DOES NOT KNOW ANYTHING ELSE THAN ONE'S PRESENT ENVIRONMENT. This is especially so when one is growing up as an unbeliever in a family of unbelievers, for then the parents are not likely to teach the children right from wrong, especially when they see all the other families allowing their kids to do the same things. To give one example here, when I was growing up in the fifties, homosexuality was actually a crime on the books of all nations on earth, and a couple living together was unheard of. Now compare that to today, three generations later, and now the current generation, thinking again of the unbelievers of the world, think these things are acceptable and NORMAL!

And so, we are to see that what we thought was normal before March 11, 2020, was really not normal at all, but rather we were all blind to the downward spiral towards hell that all countries on earth were heading toward. So what has happened to change that is that THE DEVIL NO LONGER OPERATES IN THE SHADOWS, BUT RATHER IN THE OPEN FOR ALL TO SEE, AS HIS TIME OF ACHIEVING HIS GOAL QUICKLY APPROACHES! Those who are wishing to return to a normal are in fact wishing to return to a time when all was an illusion of normalcy, while in reality the devil was simply moving the nations of the world – ever so slowly –

toward the fulfillment of his agenda of bringing in a one world government ruled by his antichrist!

"I would have despaired unless I had believed that I would see the goodness of the Lord in the land of the living."

Psalm 27:13

"For You have delivered my soul from death, indeed my feet from stumbling, so that I may walk before God in the light of the living."

Psalm 56:13

CHAPTER THREE

A personal word of testimony regarding my current life situation!

In this chapter, I would like to give readers a personal word of testimony regarding my current situation, with my reason for doing so being to convince readers that if God – Who has no favorites – can do this for me, then He is more than willing and able to do the same for any other of His children yet on earth! And here I will only use two examples from my life, one dating back to 2008 and dealing with finances, and the other dating back to 2017 and dealing with my health.

So let us begin with the first example, which relates to FINANCES! In early September 2008, I was on my field of service that God has brought me to and have been on since October 2, 1999. I was at that time living off my savings, meaning that I was supporting myself financially out of my own funds. But God knew that up to that time in my life as a believer, I had not had to depend on Him alone for finances.

Then in September 2008, as most readers would be aware of, a financial meltdown occurred on a worldwide scale. At the time, all I had to live on was invested in the stock market and doing very well. For instance, in September 2008 I had $1900 PER MONTH coming in from my investments, so that I hardly had to touch my actual savings! I was even financially supporting a local church in Jerusalem at that time. But then the crash came and my dividends slowly started dwindling down, along with the amount of money in my portfolio. The short of this part of the story here is that by the time 2012 came around, I had lost or had used up all my savings, for each month I had to sell shares in order to pay for rent, food, gas, insurance, etc. So by the time I turned 65 in 2015, I owed $15,000 on my credit cards and only had my government pension to live on!

What made matters worse was that I owned an investment property in Texas and also in Florida that I had purchased in my younger years, and while working fulltime. I ended up losing that property in Texas in early 2009 due to supposedly not paying my taxes, which was of course not true, but I did not have the financial resources to go to Texas to hire a lawyer and to fight this in court, which would have ended up costing me more than what the property was worth. I was convinced at the time that there was a scam going on there in Texas at the time, and it hurt not to be able to fight it. Nobody likes saying ‘goodbye’ to an investment worth $25,000.

I also had to sell that property in Florida at a loss in 2010, because I needed money to live on. Then I got hit with another unexpected whammy, in that my landlord raised the rent by $100 per month in February 2009, which up to then had only been going up $25 per month each year! I can assure readers that this was a very stressful time in my life! But what I did not realize at the time is that God was simply bringing me to the place of relying on Him for my every need, which included finances!

From 2012 onward, I had thoughts of getting a job, but God kept putting a stop to that every time I moved in that direction. What He was telling me was that being called to full time service as an evangelist meant that I was in DIRECT SERVICE TO HIM, which therefore meant that I WAS TO LOOK TO HIM ALONE TO MEET MY FINANCAL NEEDS, which He knew I never had to do before!

Now that God had me where He wanted me, He could now start working in a way that only God can! The first thing that happened is that in 2015 one of the banks that I was dealing with sent me an offer out of the blue, which was that I could borrow up to $5,000 with a 1% fee at 1% interest, with the money not having to be paid back for 10 months! As one can guess, I jumped at this offer, which was repeated at least three times until my full debt was paid off.

What also happened around the same time in 2015 is that another bank I was dealing with called me up and offered me a $5,000 line of credit, which was to be unsecured, since I had no assets. The interest rate was to be prime plus 2%, which it still is today. The only thing that both banks went on was that I had an excellent credit rating, 861 out 900, which I believe is even higher today! Not long after this, God moved a Christian friend to loan me $4,000 at no interest and to be paid back as I could. What this all meant then is that by the time 2020 rolled around, I was debt free, including having paid by friend back! So what I learned through this painful experience is that GOD WAS THERE TO SEE ME THROUGH! ALL I HAD TO DO WAS TRUST HIM!

I had now learned to live as cheaply as one can, meaning also learning to live on second hand clothing and footwear! I can honestly say that I identified with what the apostle Paul was led of God to write at Philippians 4:11-13 in part, "[11] ...I have learned to be content in whatever circumstances I am. [12] I know how to get along with humble means, and I also know how to live in prosperity; in any and every circumstance I have learned the secret of being filled and going hungry, both of having abundance and suffering need. [13] I can do all things through Him who strengthens me."

And now let us go on to that second example, which relates to MY HEALTH, which God knew was the only other area of my life that I never had to rely on Him alone for! And so, in the latter part of 2016, both my legs started swelling up to twice their size, including my stomach, which meant that fluid was backing up. I also started to lose bladder control at night time, which was especially difficult. Before long I was using old T-shirts that I was not using as a diaper to prevent soiling the bed sheets..

When I finally went to the doctor, not only was my PSA at 20 (doctors usually consider you to have prostate cancer if your reading is about 3:5 and higher), but an ultrasound showed that my kidneys were about to shut down, due to urine already backing up in them. My blood pressure was also up close to 200! So this was now a serious situation and there was no time to lose. I was brought to one of the nearest hospitals by ambulance and had a prostate operation done on April 1, 2017, which was a Saturday.

I was discharged from the hospital on the Tuesday evening and within a week both legs were back to normal, and I had full bladder control again at night. But the best news was that the pathology report showed no cancer was found from the material that they took out from the prostate, even though two doctors had told me before the operation that they were sure that I did have prostate cancer, due to my PSA (Prostate Specific Antigen) being 20. In any case, I just trusted God that all was now okay and I could resume my ministry in a more normal fashion.

Then in late January 2019, I woke up one morning and my left leg was swollen to twice its normal size. I knew, based on my previous experience, that the prostate was likely acting up again. So I scheduled an appointment with my family doctor and after doing blood work, discovered that my PSA reading was now 27. So he scheduled an appointment with a Urologist.

When I finally got in the summer of 2019, he wanted to do a biopsy of the prostate, as my PSA was now 33. . From all that I had read about that procedure up to that time, I simply declined. Another reason for declining was that the pathology report of 2017 had showed no cancer. And I knew that there were other factors, such as no sex, which could account for a high reading. So I just continued on with my ministry, leaving aside any thoughts about my prostate, even though my left leg was still swollen. But I had good bladder control and could urinate okay.

Then on July 8, 2021, I started urinating blood and so immediately went to Emergency, where they did all kinds of tests, discovering that my PSA was not only now 108, but that there was a tumor on the inside wall of my bladder. They discharged me with a urinary catheter and then brought me back in for a double operation on July 23, 2021, one for the prostate and other to remove the tumor in the bladder. This time the pathology report showed that there was CANCER IN BOTH THE PROSTATE AND THE BLADDER! My Urologist then scheduled a full body bone scan, and in mid-August they told me that the cancer had spread to my bones, from the thighs, all around the torso area, the rib cage, and right up to my shoulder blades on the right side. The Urologist also told me at the time that the cancer was now STAGE FOUR!

And so my immediate reaction, after getting off the phone with the doctor, was to have a time of prayer with God, asking Him, "Now what?" One thing I knew was that this was not due to sin. Not that I had never sinned, but I knew that God had not allowed this cancer due to some sin in my life. Then secondly, I came to the realization that God had NOT given me over to death, and that I had the freedom to seek alternative cancer treatments.

So after telling family and friends, I started to look for an alternative cancer clinic, for I did not believe in, nor trust, the medical establishment with their protocol. The first clinic that I wanted to go to was in Texas, but the cost would be upwards of $70,000 to $100,000 for their course of treatment. Then I quickly realized that this was completely out of my reach, for after putting out feelers, and looking to God to supply if He wanted me to go there, I got no positive response form family or friends.

Then I went to second cheaper alternative that would cost $18,000 for their course of treatment. And after putting out feelers, and looking to God to again provide if He was allowing this, I was able to raise $18,000, which included my $5,000 line of credit that I still had, and $2,000 of my own savings, and also a $5,000 no interest loan from that same friend who had loaned me the $4,000 years before. So that meant that $6,000 in hard cash was raised, which came from one sister (I have four sisters and two brothers), one niece, and two other Christian friends!

Now, because this cancer clinic that I had contacted and was now scheduled to go to for the month of September 2021 was in another city about a thousand miles away, I had flight costs to go and come back, plus accommodation and meal costs for the month I was to be away undergoing the alternative cancer treatments. What really helped here is that the cancer clinic set me up with a manor for the aged a few blocks away, where I was able to stay fairly cheaply. So when I added all the costs up, the total when I got back home was $20,400! I was able to secure a $3,000 loan from the bank where I have the line of credit, and have at the time of writing paid that back, which means that I now owe my friend $5,000 and about $4,600 on my line of credit, which is still prime plus 2%.

There are TWO THINGS that it is important for readers to know before we go any further. The FIRST relates to the fact that up to that point in my life I had lost my mother, my wife, some first cousins, and some close personal friends to cancer, with ALL OF THEM having gone by way of chemotherapy, radiation, and operations! So I had come to the conclusion that the conventional methods of treating cancer were NOT CURING cancer, but only fighting the disease until one died. And of course making a lot of money for the pharmaceutical companies in the process, while providing a ready supply of patients to the health care industry!

And please realize that this is not being said here out of hatred or bitterness for the healthcare system due to those I have lost to that system of care, but it was discovered, while doing the research for one of my books, that starting with the Flexner Report in 1910 in the US, there was a concerted effort made, which succeeded, in shutting down all medical schools in the US and Canada which utilized medical practices derived from natural means!

One should know here that in those days, there were many cures for cancer, in that many people were actually cured through diet and various natural supplements! However, as the pharmaceutical industry gained a foothold and 'unapproved' medical schools were being shut down, all these cures were labeled as quackery and the medical doctors involved either lost their license to practice, or were sued by the new emerging medical establishment until they shut down their practices! So please be aware dear readers that the healthcare industry is foremost of all A BUSINESS, and it needs a ready supply of patients to turn a profit! If you are not convinced of this, please do some research! I recommend alternative sites such as bitchute.com, where there is no censoring, and also the search engine duckduckgo.com.

Let me give you a very practical example here, which is the TREATMENT PLAN that my Urologist came up with and the one that the alternative cancer doctor came up with. What my Urologist specified is hormonal therapy, which seeks to lower testosterone levels to zero, which in turn lowers the PSA reading to almost nil. But this is not without serious side effects. Then they add drugs that seek to prevent the cancer from finding other pathways; but there are very serious side effects to these drugs, so that one is more likely to die from the drugs than the cancer!

Now, in the case of the alternative cancer doctor, here is his TREATMENT PLAN. First, through the anti-cancer supplements, he seeks to stop the spread of the cancer to go any further. Once that is achieved, and one marker for this having been achieved is the PSA test. Then the second step is to get the cancer to regress. This can be determined through a bone scan, for instance, to see if the bone cancer has spread or regressed. And the third step, which is really started as part of the first step, is to build up THE IMMUNE SYSTEM so that one's own body is fighting the cancer. A lot of this is achieved through an anti-cancer diet. Once one's immune system has been built up, then this helps the anti-cancer supplements to be even more effective. It is this third step that I encouraged my Urologist to incorporate into his practice; but by his reaction, I know that what I said went in one ear and out the other! And it is such a reaction as this which leads me to realize that I need to be proactive in taking responsibility for my health, and not leave that up to a doctor, no matter how qualified one might be on paper!

It is important to keep in mind here that God so designed these bodies so that when the proper functioning of the body is achieved, then it can work to heal itself! So I ask you, dear readers, if you were in my place, would you also have gone to see an alternative cancer doctor?

Then the second important thing which needs to be mentioned here is what God says in His word about health, and therefore what my conviction has come to be regarding health! For instance, at Exodus 15:26, we read in God's word, "And He (God) said, "If you will give earnest heed to the voice of the Lord your God, and do what is right in His sight, and give ear to His commandments, and keep all His statutes, I WILL PUT NONE OF THE DISEASES ON YOU WHICH I HAVE PUT on the Egyptians (representing unbelievers); FOR I, THE LORD, AM YOUR HEALER (speaking this to believers)." We clearly see here that one's spiritual condition vis-a-vis God determines one's physical condition in this world, in terms of being free from disease and sickness!

This does not of course mean that a believer is never sick or never incurs a disease, since we are human beings that are indwelt with a sinful nature that always wants to lead us into sin, even after salvation. This therefore means that God at times needs to apply some strong medicine to those who are His children through salvation, which includes allowing whatever it takes to bring a child of His back on track with Him! I do recall being brought to 'the wood shed' more than once by my earthly father, whenever he thought that I needed it!

Then other times where God might allow sickness or disease is to bring a child of His home, speaking here of when one's life journey has ended and one will now die physically! Then there are also cases where God will allow a sickness or disease in order to bring His child into an even closer relationship with Him, in terms of totally depending on Him; or in terms of wanting to accomplish something through His child, with God choosing to do so through a sickness or disease!

For instance, years ago there was a godly woman in our local fellowship who fell ill and found herself in the hospital. Part of my ministry at that time was visiting the sick in the hospital, and so I went to visit her one evening. She was in a room with another woman, so we were not alone. In talking with her, I discovered that one issue she had was the fact that her husband was unsaved and so she was not submitting to his authority in the home. I read her a passage of Scripture on this matter, in which I encouraged her to submit to her husband for the sake of the gospel. And so, after we had a word of prayer, I left.

The following Sunday, she was attending the worship service with us and had the woman with her who had been in the same room. And it was announced that our godly woman had led her to faith in God while there, and almost immediately her sickness had left her and she was discharged from the hospital! And not too long after this, her husband, who had never attended with us, started attending the services!

So what I learned from that experience is that this godly woman had only been allowed by God to fall ill in order to be admitted to the hospital, because God knew that there was a precious soul that was already there, who was ready to be saved! And of course, God used the occasion for her to receive some needed counsel so that she might honor God in her home, and when she did, then God used that to start speaking to her husband about his spiritual condition!

In now coming back to my current situation, at the time of writing this – which is now almost thirteen months since being diagnosed with fourth stage cancer – I have been able to carry on my ministry as evangelist, author, and counselor, just as I was doing before I was diagnosed with the cancer, and what is amazing – for which I give God thanks for – is that I am able to function normally without any pain medication whatsoever! I hear that bone cancer is normally one of the most painful cancers one can have, yet I am relatively pain-free! Whenever a pain does come up, which is often, I immediately go to God and ask Him to heal, and it is gone!

I told one of my sisters not too long ago that I believed that God has told this cancer that it could go so far and not any further. For what needs to be grasped here is that when the cancer spread from the prostate to the bladder; it then had two pathways that it could take, either go to the bones, or go to the lymphatic system, or do both. In my case, it has so far only gone to the bones. But what is amazing here is that the rib cage, where the cancer is, is also connected to the spinal cord, so that so far, there is no indication that the cancer has gone there, for if it does, then I could quickly lose mobility and be confined to a wheelchair, or it could go to the brain and I might not have long after that. And the rib cage is also touching all the major organs, and as far as we know, there has not been any crossover there either! Thank God!

The alternative cancer doctor did talk me into taking the hormonal therapy from my Urologist, which I am presently on. This consists of an injection into the stomach lining every four months, but this has a lot of side effects, the worse being to increase one's probability of a heart attack or stroke by 50% for anyone above 70. I am 72. The Urologist tried to start me on another drug a few months ago that is designed to try to prevent the cancer from going into other pathways, but I declined this drug after reading the medical information that came with the bottle. For instance, under "very common occurrences," here is what it actually says, "fractured bones, in all cases." Then under "common occurrences," it read, "heart attack, heart disease, and heart failure!" No thank you! I am now praying to God for some way to even get off the hormone therapy!

When I was at the alternative cancer clinic, the doctor put me on five anti-cancer supplements that I am still taking, plus I have added a few more since then after discovering a list of 20 of them from a Urologist that believes in alternative cancer treatments. I have also revised the way I eat and have been following a diet consisting of mostly anti-cancer foods. I will have more to say on this in the next chapter.

What I want to leave readers with here is the fact that by the grace of God I have been able to carry on my ministry same as before the cancer diagnosis, and also all chores associated with living on one's own. So the point here is that if God is able to do this for me – and again, God has no favorites – then He is able to provide for each one of you at the moment, no matter what your situation happens to be!

O yes, I almost forgot, I have now come to the conclusion that God allowed His servant to have this cancer because there are things that He wanted to accomplish in and through my life, so that He determined this was the best way to achieve it! I have already mentioned that I have drawn much closer to God than I have ever been in my life as a child of His, which now spans almost 43 years. And there are also a number of people that I am praying for now that I believe will one day be in Heaven.

Four of those people relate to my stay in the hospital over those four days, when I had the double operation, and then there are eight people that I am praying for relating to my trip to that alternative cancer clinic, for in both cases, God did provide opportunities to share the gospel, which is God's good news relating to what He has done for humankind during the ages of time through His Beloved Son, especially His death for our sins, His burial to put those sins away, and His resurrection from the dead the third day, and His subsequent ascension back to His Father's right Hand; for it is through His Son as alive forevermore by The Holy Spirit that God now imparts His eternal life for one to live by, who believes in Him for salvation! So to God be the praise, the honor, and the glory, both now and forevermore! Amen.

“let it be known to all of you and to all the people of Israel, that by the name of Jesus Christ the Nazarene, whom you crucified, whom God raised from the dead — by this name this man stands here before you in good health.”

Acts 4:10

“Beloved, I pray that in all respects you may prosper and be in good health, just as your soul prospers.”

3 John 1:2

CHAPTER FOUR

Our health is our responsibility!

A few years ago, the family doctor I was going to at the time had a sign in his office which read, "Your health is your responsibility. I am simply here to help you achieve it!" He turned out to not be that good of a doctor, but at least he did subscribe to a good philosophy for his practice! And this is now the truth that we all need to adhere to, which is to take responsibility for our own health, if we are not already doing so, and not leave that vital step in the hands of someone else, including the medical profession!

For the reality to be grasped is that medical doctors ARE financially compensated by the pharmaceutical companies for every prescription they write, and they are also handsomely compensated for every surgery they perform, and every test they prescribe. This is not being written to have someone stop going to a medical professional, but rather to have people stop placing these folks on a pedestal, as if they know more about you, or care more about you, than you do!

And so, one thing I would recommend as a first step is to request all health records after each test and procedure performed, which they are required by law to provide if requested. More than once I have been surprised to see things written there that I was not aware of, such as a comment by another doctor, or a reading that the doctor did not mention when giving me the results, which has then proven to be important for my wellbeing! So please always request your records!

What is also important is to not wait to be told by a doctor to stop smoking or drinking, if one is doing so at present, FOR BOTH OF THESE ARE CANCER-PRODUCING! It may take a few years, but both of these practices will probably eventually kill you. Most people are aware of the adverse effects from smoking, but few are relating to alcohol, or any drug for that matter, such as marijuana. Please do your own research on alcohol consumption and its relation to cancer. You will be surprised.

Before God saved my soul on January 14, 1980, I used to be a heavy drinker and smoker. The smoking was given up a month or two before being saved due to picking up a leaflet from the cancer society in the doctor's office and reading it while waiting for my appointment. In it, I discovered that there was a whole list of chemicals contained in the tobacco and the smoke which never leaves one's body after being inhaled, but becomes imbedded in the organs, especially the lungs, with many of those compounds being carcinogenic, that is, cancer-producing! That was enough to have me quit smoking cold-turkey from that moment on! The desire for alcohol fell off about three months after being saved and never returned!

The next most important thing that one can do in taking responsibility for one's own health is to be careful of the food one eats! A lot of people are not aware of the importance of food in relation to one's health. And here, it is important to avoid all GMO (Genetically Modified Organism) foods. Our bodies do not easily – if at all – digest any compounds made in a laboratory. God intended us to get our food from the ground, not the lab! Again, please do your own research on this, as you will be surprised at all the gastrointestinal problems that have cropped up since these GMO products were introduced. GMO products are nothing more than a money-making ploy, as the seeds of plants genetically-modified can then be patented, which then forces the farmers to buy these seeds from the manufacturer holding these patents! If at all possible, please buy ORGANIC whenever possible. The cost is not that much more, in most cases.

Another very important recommendation here is to not forget EXERCISE, for this has almost as much importance to one maintaining a good immune system, as one's diet does! The exercise one does here will depend on whether one is a male or female; whether one is older or younger; and will also depend on one's health condition. In my case, even at 72 and with fourth stage cancer, I do about 700 stair steps each day; I try to have a 20 minute walk outside each day; I do stretch exercises three time each day; I do ten minutes of lifting two five pound weights six days a week; and I am on a treadmill for six minutes five times each day! I still also continue to do my own housecleaning and yardwork.

One positive result of this exercise is to keep my weight the same month after month, year after year, and it also enables me to have a good appetite, and to sleep well at night, including regular bowel movements. I have found that I need nine hours sleep each night, and I have to get up twice to go to the bathroom. After that first time up to go to the bathroom each night I take an 8 mg melatonin tablet in order to help me fall back asleep. The melatonin is also helps fight the cancer!

Another very important piece of health information that readers need to be aware of is the harmful effects of exposure to electromagnetic frequency (EMF) radiation, especially from cell phones and cell phone towers where there is 5G installed! If this is the first time that you hear about this, then PLEASE DO SOME RESEARCH, as this is deathly serious! Two source for information on this is as noted previously, with one being the website bitchute.com and the other being the search engine, duckduckgo.com!

The city that I went to for my alternative cancer treatments was full of 5G towers, and I tried to avoid them like the plague! There are also shields that one can buy for one's cell phone to help protect one when not in use. This is again one more of those things that is being hidden from the general public!

I was going to make mention of the vaccines that are available for the so-called 'C-19 pandemic,' but since by this time one is either unvaccinated, as I am, or vaccinated, whether one followed the advice of one's doctor, or one was forced in order to keep one's employment. But whatever you do here, it is highly recommended that one does some research on this topic, as all these vaccines are experimental and for emergency use only, with many serious side effects being reported worldwide! The reason one is not being pointed toward sites like YouTube, Google, Facebook (Meta), and Instagram, is that these sites suppress or shield you from the truth regarding these vaccines. These sites DO NOT have your best interest at heart, and do not stand for the truth, but rather exist only to push a certain agenda!

“Let all bitterness and wrath and anger and clamor and slander be put away from you, along with all malice. Be kind to one another, tender-hearted, forgiving each other, just as God in Christ also has forgiven you.”

Ephesians 4:31,32

“So, as those who have been chosen of God, holy and beloved, put on a heart of compassion, kindness, humility, gentleness and patience; bearing with one another, and forgiving each other, whoever has a complaint against anyone; just as the Lord forgave you, so also should you.”

Colossians 3:12,13

CHAPTER FIVE

We all have to learn to forgive and move on!

During my life as a believer over these last forty-two plus years, I have encountered many people, both believers and unbelievers, who have become angry, bitter, and soured on life due to some person, experience, or situation, which they have encountered in the course of living. And the unfortunate fact is that this has caused these individuals to either become physically sick, or mentally ill, or both, as a result!

For what we all need to grasp here is that anger and bitterness are like a cancer within, in that if left undealt with, it soon affects one's whole being, and always to the detriment of the person affected! It is therefore imperative that one learn to deal with anger and bitterness in one's life, in order to be spared some more serious consequences, even to adversely affect all one's relationships, and even one's employment!

What we all need to realize, especially in the days that we are presently in, is that this is not only a world full of fallen people, but it is also a world where evil is on full display! And if we add on top of that what the people of this world have been subjected to the last two plus years, then there are a lot of broken-down people, mentally, physically, emotionally, and financially; which has also meant that the companies where these people are employed are most certainly not functioning in a 'normal' fashion by any stretch of the imagination!

What this means then is that there are many people, events, and circumstances out there, that we are confronted with each day, which, if we allow them to, can lead us to become angry and then bitter! That is why we all need to take a step back and stop adding fuel to the fire by learning to DEAL WITH OUR REACTIONS to those people, events, or circumstances in a constructive way, so that we do not become incapacitated. If we are a parent with children, then those children are depending on us! And if we are a grandparent, then our children and grandchildren are looking to us for how to handle the unpleasantness's of this life, and so we need to be there to show them the way!

It is therefore imperative that if one is a believer, that one put in practice in one's life the practical solutions that God offers us in His word! God not only designed and created us, but He also gave us the manual, the Bible, for how to live on earth, under the best and the worst of times! So what God says should be the first step in dealing with any problem we encounter in this life. Let us note for instance what God says at Psalm 34:19, "Many are the afflictions of the righteous, but the Lord delivers him out of them all." That is most certainly true, but only when we are cooperating with Him! You can lead a horse to water that is available to quench the horse's thirst, but unless the horse drinks of that water, the poor animal will remain thirsty!

And so with us, we need to see that anger and bitterness results and remains ONLY WHEN WE ARE UNWILLING TO FORGIVE AND THEN MOVE ON! The longer we wait to do so, the harder it becomes to forgive and move on, for then we are building tracks within ourselves for our reactions to travel on in the future! In other words, we are giving our reactions a ready pattern from the past to use in the future, on how to handle all such people, events, and circumstances!

What I counsel people to do when faced with anger in themselves, leading to bitterness, is to immediately say to God, "Father, I forgive that person (for every unpleasant situation or circumstance almost always involves people), I ask you to forgive that person (and it is important to name the person by name), and please deal with my feelings toward that person, and also with that person! And then every time that person, event, or circumstance comes to mind again, one simply needs to take that thought captive and give it to God!

For what we all need to realize is that unforgiveness is a sin, and when left undealt with it means that we are continuing on in that sin, and the result is to continue in the anger and bitterness that has arisen and taken hold, because one is unwilling to forgive and move on! These are not easy times for sure, as all can testify to; but we do not have to make them any more difficult than they are by being part of the problem, instead of opting for the solution, which is to forgive and move on!

In closing this chapter, let me give a practical example. I have a neighbor, who has been my neighbor for 21 years. He is single (by choice) and is 60 and now retired. Three years ago, he lost his job, as the Company he was with underwent a downsizing; but thankfully for him he did receive a generous severance package. As a result of losing his job, he became angry and very bitter, and became still more bitter the following year, when the WHO (World Health Organization) announced a worldwide 'pandemic,' which resulted in a worldwide shutdown. Since he has always been very well off financially, he had been in the habit of taking multiple vacations each year. In fact, I used to joke that he was never home!

I had a few talks with him in the spring of 2020, trying to help him overcome his anger and bitterness and deal with the world as it is, and not as he wanted it to be. But I soon had to give up, for I realized that he was not only becoming unresponsive to my counsel, but that he was getting delusional and mentally unstable. And since that time, he most certainly has not gotten any better!

This is also a man that I have shared the gospel with, have given him a New Testament, and later a full Bible. He is aware that I have a service in my home (rental unit) every Sunday, which he respects, for instance, by not having any music on, or making any type of noise whatsoever, such as a lawnmower.

But what has happened since the fall of 2020 is that he has started to show hatred toward me, being very abusive verbally each time he sees me; then escalating this to try to physically prevent my movements when going on my walks, at first doing so with his body, and then doing so with his truck. Then he went even further by starting to utter a death threat, and when he did so, I called the police, who came and talked to him. But since I did not have a video record of this, nor could I provide witnesses, then they said there was nothing they could do, as it was my word against his, as he simply denied everything.

Then when he physically assaulted me one evening while on my walk, I called the police again, and it was the same story again, I had no concrete proof, in terms of witnesses, and it was again his word against mine, as he again denied doing so. At that point, I simply resolved that I was never again going to call the police, but simply rely on God in the future to be my protection, as I am very much aware of His promise at Psalm 23:4, where we read, “Even though I walk through the valley of the shadow of death, I fear no evil, for You are with me; Your rod and Your staff, they comfort me,” and also God’s promise at Psalm 50:15, where we read, “Call upon Me in the day of trouble; I shall rescue you, and you will honor Me." These are two verses that I have used often when I have been afraid.

And so, the short of the story is that even to the time of writing, every time he sees me, he yells out, “Hey pedophile, how many children have you molested today?,” or “What was it like when you were in prison?” and so forth. He has even kept his truck running with the exhaust near my garage and filled it with exhaust fumes when he knew I was in there. And on and on.

The point in relating this is to show that this is the type of situation where it would be easy to be angry at the guy and to have bitter feelings toward him. In fact, from a purely human perspective, many might even say that I would be justified.

However, as a minister and counselor, God has taught me otherwise, so that every time he does or says something that could cause me to react with anger and bitterness, I have learnt to simply ask God to forgive him, letting God know that I have also forgiven him, and also asking God to deal with my feelings toward him, and to also deal with him.

For as an evangelist, I know that if God were to save him, then that would turn an enemy into a friend! And so, that is why I pray for him in my morning and evening prayers, asking God to deliver him from the power of the evil one and to bring him into the kingdom of His beloved Son, in whom there is redemption, the forgiveness of sins (which is Colossians 1:12-14). In this way, I do not give the devil a foothold into my life through sin, thereby allowing God's love to continue to flow through me! In this way I am able to continue to please God, instead of pleasing the devil through anger, bitterness, and unforgiveness! Trusting this short word of testimony has been helpful in your own daily walk!

"For by grace you have been saved through faith; and that not of yourselves, it is the gift of God; not as a result of works, so that no one may boast. For we are His workmanship, created in Christ Jesus for good works, which God prepared beforehand so that we would walk in them."

Ephesians 2:8-10

"But when the kindness of God our Savior and His love for mankind appeared, He saved us, not on the basis of deeds which we have done in righteousness, but according to His mercy, by the washing of regeneration and renewing by the Holy Spirit, whom He poured out upon us richly through Jesus Christ our Savior, so that being justified by His grace we would be made heirs according to the hope of eternal life."

Titus 3:4-7

"Therefore, since Christ has suffered in the flesh, arm yourselves also with the same purpose, because he who has suffered in the flesh has ceased from sin, so as to live the rest of the time in the flesh no longer for the lusts of men, but for the will of God."

1 Peter 4:1,2

CHAPTER SIX

We have been saved in order to only serve God after salvation!

What we will do on this chapter is touch upon the truth for why God saved each one of us reading this, who are now privileged to know God in salvation! How critical that we see that God saved each one of us in order that one might only serve God after salvation! Let us relate this to an example from our physical lives in order to see why this has to be so.

Many reading this are likely parents, which means that God has allowed you to either be a father or a mother of a precious child born into this world. Now let us say that as soon as the child grows up; the child starts to serve only the neighbor next door; mowing his lawn, taking out his garbage, and whatever chores the neighbor might give to your child. Now you are the one who gave this child birth into this world, feeds, clothes, and provides shelter for that child, yet the child never serves you! After a while you might start to wonder if that child actually belongs to your neighbor, and not to you! And so, God is not being unreasonable to expect those whom He has saved to only render service to Him after salvation. If one does not, then it would be reasonable to conclude that one might not be a child of His at all, that is, that one has never really experienced God's salvation at all!

What I would now like to do in the rest of this chapter is give readers SIX REASONS why we need serve God after salvation. As a minister, I am also aware that often, one is not serving God because one has never been taught how to serve God after salvation. And so, before we look at these six reasons for why we need to serve God, we need to grasp the fact that before salvation, we used to serve our own selves, for we were unbelievers and did not know God, so could not serve Him.

So what happens at salvation is that God not only forgives all of our sins, but He also imparts to us the very eternal life that He Himself ever lives, doing so by His Holy Spirit coming to indwell us. And so, after salvation we will be serving God, by carrying on His will on earth when we live by His imparted life! And we will be living by His imparted life automatically as we live with no known unconfessed sins in our lives! That is why God gives believers the only confessional they will ever need after salvation, which is 1 John 1:9, where we read, “If we confess our sins, He is faithful and righteous to forgive us our sins and to cleanse us from all unrighteousness.” And now, let us go on to those six reasons why we need to be serving God in a world with no normal:

1) We need to serve God because He saved us so that we would willingly serve Him out of love for Him!

The reason that God saved us in order that we would willingly serve Him out of love for Him is due to the fact that God created mankind originally in order that we would all serve Him willingly out of love for Him, and now through salvation, He is simply bringing us back to His original design! Through the entrance of sin into God’s original sinless creation, all humanity turned from God and in the process “all of us like sheep have gone astray, each of us has turned to his own way” (Isaiah 53:6), which in reality meant that instead of serving God, for which we had all been created to do, we served ourselves, doing our own will instead of God’s will.

And had God not intervened to save some for Himself, we would all have willingly stayed away from Him, doing our own thing, content in our pride, but nevertheless on our way to a lost eternity knowingly or unknowingly. But God in His mercy and grace gave some of us the gift of life, which we did not deserve, noting these tremendous words at Ephesians 2:8-10, "[8] For by grace you have been saved through faith; and that not of yourselves, it is the gift of God; [9] not as a result of works, so that no one may boast. [10] For we are His workmanship, created in Christ Jesus for good works, which God prepared beforehand so that we would walk in them." So the truth to remember here is that God saved us, as a gift of His mercy and grace, so that we would willingly serve Him out of love for Him after we had come to know Him in a personal relationship at salvation!

Another truth which is important to grasp and remember here is that God never forces Himself upon anyone. Yes, it is true that He is in us to work out His will in accordance with His good pleasure (noting Philippians 2:13), but He desires to work with us with our eyes fully open to what He is doing, so that we are in full assent of what He is doing in us and through us. There is true blessing for us in not only seeing God at work in our lives, but in also seeing what He is doing. All God does is out of love for us so that the more we see God's Hand at work in us and through us, the more we come to realize just how much He loves us!

Therefore, it is in this light that we now need to view what God says to His believers at 2 Corinthians 5:14,15, where we read, "[14] For the love of Christ controls us, having concluded this, that one died for all, therefore all died; [15] and He died for all, so that they who live might no longer live for themselves, but for Him who died and rose again on their behalf." At verse 15, God clearly states that "those who live," this being all human beings who come to experience His salvation in time as a gift from Him, are no longer to "live for themselves, but for Him Who died and rose again on their behalf." And to live for Him here means to serve Him willingly out of love for Him!

2] We need to serve God because our wellbeing depends on our serving God!

One of the greatest tragedies in life is the tremendous amount of lost potential that exists in the human race. People are highly educated and yet are not working at the level for which they were trained, either through lack of employment in one's field, or through lack of opportunity or advancement where one is working. Women were created by God for the prime purpose of bearing children, but through lack of suitable mates, through career choices, or because of a spouse who does not want children, one is left childless. A son or daughter has tremendous potential as an artist or a musician, but because the parents had always dreamed of their children following in their footsteps, they are denied the opportunity to develop their true potential in those areas.

Similarly in the physical world, we do not buy a car, or a stove, or a fridge, just to have these appliances sit where they are placed without being used. And even in nature, God well utilizes everything that He has created, for everything was created for a purpose, whether that be the sun, the wind, the rain, the clouds, or anything else that exists of what we can see. Even every creature on the food chain is there for a purpose, either to be a meal for another creature, or else for man's enjoyment and provision.

Therefore, the irony to be observed is that God created human beings for His purpose and enjoyment, and all we have done since creation is bring Him grief, through our continual rebellion and sin! And relating to our present subject, we are to see that we were actually created to serve God, yet due to sin, we as a human race have preferred to serve the creature rather than The Creator, noting what God tells us at Romans 1:25 in part, "For they exchanged the truth of God for a lie, and worshiped and served the creature rather than the Creator..."

The best way to describe a life that is out of sort with its intended purpose is to use the word 'misery.' One is miserable from the time one gets up in the morning until one goes to bed at night, day in and day out, even though one tries to numb that pain through drugs, alcohol, smoking, or sex. Even as a child of God, if one is not serving God after coming to know Him in a personal relationship at salvation, then one is also miserable.

One cannot live with one's self or with others. Only when we serve the purpose for which we were created and then saved by God for, which is to serve Him willingly out of love for Him, do we find true heart rest, with the peace and joy that can only be found in being at the place God intends for us. Therefore, it cannot be emphasized enough that our wellbeing, especially as children of God still on earth, depends on our serving God!

As one example of many which could be given that our wellbeing in this life depends on our serving God, please note what God says at Deuteronomy 11:13-17, where we read, "[13] It shall come about, if you listen obediently to my commandments which I am commanding you today, to love the Lord your God and to serve Him with all your heart and all your soul, [14] that He will give the rain for your land in its season, the early and late rain, that you may gather in your grain and your new wine and your oil. [15] He will give grass in your fields for your cattle, and you will eat and be satisfied. [16] Beware that your hearts are not deceived, and that you do not turn away and serve other gods and worship them. [17] Or the anger of the Lord will be kindled against you, and He will shut up the heavens so that there will be no rain and the ground will not yield its fruit; and you will perish quickly from the good land which the Lord is giving you."

What is very important to grasp here is that to not serve God because one is an unbeliever is understandable, because such are in rebellion against God and are suffering a miserable existence because of it. However, to know God personally and to not serve Him is also an act of rebellion and God needs to act as any loving parent would do toward their own children. His Hand will be against such rebellious children until one does serve Him willingly out of love for Him, or else He with take such a child home through physical death.

But please ever remember that God is not seeking service from us because He needs it, far from it, but because He knows that He has designed us in such a way as to only find our greatest contentment in serving Him. And the only person who will ever scoff at what has just been said is the person who has never served Him! Notice here what God says serving Him is like, which is really the doing of His will, noting what He says about this at Romans 12:2, "And do not be conformed to this world, but be transformed by the renewing of your mind, so that you may prove what the will of God is, that which is good and acceptable and perfect."

That "which is good and acceptable and perfect," being what God says we will find in doing God's will. In other words, what cannot be improved upon. And so, once we have served God by doing His will, then we see that it was indeed good and acceptable and perfect. One cannot even describe the sense of wellbeing one experiences except to know within ourselves that we are indeed glad to have served God by carrying out His will. After all, God is not seeking our service when He asks for our service, but rather He is seeking our greatest wellbeing, which He knows can only come in serving Him!

3) We need to serve God because there is yet work to be done!

Another reason for serving God after coming to know Him is that there is still work to be done, or else we would not be here. One reason for God saving us was that we might serve Him, as we have seen already. Another reason for God wanting us to serve Him after saving us is because He has work for us to do as a child of His. We often do not realize that all of our life before we even knew God in a personal relationship was shaped by God in such a way so as to be the vessel He would later use once we did come to known Him at salvation! With God, absolutely everything has a place and a purpose.

If something exists, it is because it serves some purpose of God somewhere in creation, or else it would not be in existence. It was not that long ago that medical researchers finally figured out the purpose for why we have tonsils, a gallbladder, and an appendix. Until they did, doctors were routinely removing the appendix when doing a gallbladder operation, or removing the gallbladder when removing the appendix. Same with the tonsils, they too were being removed as a matter of course, with doctors not truly being aware of what their true purpose was. But once these 'men of science' came to know why God put in tonsils, a gallbladder, and an appendix in the original design, then they were no longer being removed unless absolutely necessary, as is the case today.

We can trust God, for He knows what He is doing. So not only does God want us to serve Him because in doing so we come to experience our greatest wellbeing, but also because He has yet work for us as His children to do, both as a body of believers and individually. What is coming to a close is the present age, which is immediately followed by a time of God's judgment on earth. What God reveals in His word is that there are certain events which need to take place before this present age ends. One of those events is for all those who are to be saved by God to indeed be saved.

But what we ever need to grasp in this regard is that God delights to work through His creation in accomplishing His work, with His precious Son, The Lord Jesus Christ, being our Pattern in this while He was here on earth in human flesh. And so, in bringing in those who remain to be brought to salvation during the present age, God wants to use those who are already believers, working in us so that we will share our faith with others. Therefore, this is one very important task that God has for us to do as His children in these last days, which is to be cleansed and available vessels in His Hands, which He can use to bring the message of salvation to others!

Another very important work which supports the task just mentioned is for us as believers to love and encourage one another as brothers and sisters in the faith, while we wait for this age to end. As love for others grows cold and even non-existent in a world apart from God, it becomes even more necessary for those who personally know The Source of all love, to exhibit that love by caring for one another, encouraging one another, and supporting one another. But we will not do so, being instead a casualty rather than a blessing, if we are not walking with God as led and guided by

The Holy Spirit, living by God's imparted life, with no known unconfessed sins in our lives!

And so, in regards to the work mentioned above, that yet remains to be done, let us notice what God says to us at 2 Corinthians 6:1,2, "[1] And working together with Him, we also urge you not to receive the grace of God in vain — [2] for He says, "At the acceptable time I listened to you, and on the day of salvation I helped you." Behold, now is "the acceptable time," behold, now is "the day of salvation," and also at Hebrews 10:24,25, "[24] and let us consider how to stimulate one another to love and good deeds, [25] not forsaking our own assembling together, as is the habit of some, but encouraging one another; and all the more as you see the day drawing near." May God indeed find us doing so, by His grace and power, as we see this age draw to a close.

4) We need to serve God because it is well pleasing to Him and is always without regrets!

What parent is not pleased with an obedient child, who, when asked to do something, goes ahead and does it without complaining. While we expect and desire our children to be like that, we often forget that this is exactly what God desires from us and is what He is well pleased with once we become His children! As human beings, we have been designed by God to serve Him and to find our greatest blessing in doing so. It may be hard to believe what has just been said, especially if one is reading this as a new believer, who has only known what it is like to serve self all of one's life up to now. After serving God for the last forty-two years, I can testify that the greatest blessing that I derive out of life is in serving God. And I am not just saying this to fill a page in this book or to sell books; God is my witness that this is true!

Allow me to give a practical example here. On Saturday, February 28th, 2015, the woman who had been cutting my hair for the last eight years called. Normally I take Mondays to do my grocery shopping, banking, and other appointments. This day was the grand opening of her barber shop, where she also has two other women working for and with her. I had been aware of the opening being this particular Saturday, but since I usually do all my running around on a Monday, I was only planning to drop in on Monday to see the place and get my hair cut. But since she had called and specifically insisted that I come, then I told her I would.

So I committed the matter to God and asked Him to organize my day so as to take in this change of plans, since I normally stay at home and work Saturdays. Believe me when I say that there are no days off for a minister, as a servant of God! One thing I also remember saying to God in my spirit was why this had to occur, for we do not always like a change to our established routines. But having served God for a long time now, I know through experience that whatever He allows is always for a purpose and in order to bless us.

Besides, I have been reaching out for the last eight years to the woman who cuts my hair, even having once had her, her husband and daughter, for lunch at my home. I had therefore consented to go for the sake of the gospel, even though for me it seemed like an inconvenience. So what I ended up doing was to do that day all I normally do on a Monday.

Then at around 2 pm, having completed all I needed to do, I stopped by the barber shop. One thing that I had prayed ahead of time is for the woman who does my hair to be free once I got there, and she was. It was obvious when I walked in that she was glad to see me. And it was only then that I realized why she had wanted me to go that day, which was to meet some of the family members, who were there. Her husband and daughter were there also, whom I had not seen in quite a while. So the first half hour after getting there was spent in just meeting people and having a coffee with them, plus seeing the new place, including meeting the staff. In fact, I even had quite an extended conversation with one of the woman who works for her, even getting an opportunity to share about God and my ministry.

The short of it is that when I got home, I got down on my knees and truly thanked God for the way He had allowed this change of plans and then outworked all for His glory and my blessing. I can frankly say that I was truly blessed in my time out that day, not only being an encouragement, I am sure, to the woman who cuts my hair, but also because it was truly a beautiful day to be out, with Monday, as it turned out, had inclement weather.

And not only that, but earlier that afternoon I had also met the husband of a woman who works at one of the places I usually go to on Mondays. She did not have to work and was out with her husband. Being an evangelist, meeting people is never a coincidence and is always in the purpose of God. So as I sit here relating this, I have a smile on my face and am truly blessed for having set aside my own desires in order to serve God, by carrying out His will instead of my own.

For what needs to be grasped here is that all people, events, and circumstances are being outworked by God for our blessing when we are walking with Him under The Holy Spirit's guidance, with no known unconfessed sins in our lives, living only by God's imparted life moment by moment! What this means is that He organizes our days with what is well pleasing to Him and brings glory to Himself, to be sure, but since God is not selfish like we tend to be, He always works out of love for us and for our wellbeing in all people, events and circumstances which He allows to touch our lives each day.

The added truth to be grasped here is that we will not see this, however, until we have served Him by being willing to set aside our own plans and agendas in order to do so! Only then do we get to find out through experience the truth of Romans 12:2, where God says, "And be not conformed to this world: but be ye transformed by the renewing of your mind, that ye may prove what is that good, and acceptable, and perfect, will of God." Being conformed to this world means doing my own thing instead of being dedicated to carrying out God's will. God says to us here, 'Come do my will and only then will you find out that it is indeed good, acceptable or pleasing, and perfect, in that it cannot ever be improved upon!'

If we have lived long enough, we may start looking back over our lives and realize that there are some things that we would do differently if we had to start our lives over again. In other words, there are very few of us who can say they have lived life without regrets. While this may be true for our life while we still did not know God, this should not be true from the moment we do come to know God in a personal relationship.

For the reality to be grasped is that God wants us to avoid ever living a life with regrets. That is why to serve God is to live a life without regrets. For only then do we find true meaning for our lives and true contentment with the way our lives are being outworked. When we trust God with our lives, He outworks them in accordance with an eternal plan, which is designed only for our wellbeing, noting what God's promise to us is at Jeremiah 29:11, "For I know the plans that I have for you,' declares the Lord, 'plans for welfare and not for calamity to give you a future and a hope." And we can be sure that God's plan for our lives includes living a life that is sure to be without regrets!

The further reality, which we all need to grasp here, is that we all go through this life just once, without ever being able to relive any part of it. The truth which can be added here is that for most things in life, it is never too late. It is never too late to get that education, to get married, to start a new job, to start your own business, to tell someone you love them, to have children even in old age, if one is a man.

Before one laughs here, please consider that after Abraham's wife Sarah died, he remarried again when he was well past the age of 100. And since he had married a much younger woman, he had six sons by her (Genesis 25:1,2). Now we know that God called Abraham 'His friend' (James 2:23) many centuries after Abraham had died, so we can be sure that while Abraham lived, he lived to serve God, which we are to notice was a life without regrets. And when Abraham died, he was 175 years old.

Please note what God says to His own at Deuteronomy 5:33, "You shall walk in all the way which the Lord your God has commanded you, that you may live and that it may be well with you, and that you may prolong your days in the land which you will possess." Since Abraham lived to be 175 years old, then we can be sure that he walked with God, carrying out His will, in short, serving God while he lived. And God blessed him for it.

One of the meanings for the word 'regret' is 'annoyance concerning a thing left undone.' When we serve God by living under the leading and guidance of The Holy Spirit, living by His imparted life, with no known unconfessed sins in our lives, we can be sure that when our life ends as a child of God here on earth, that we will not be at all annoyed at anything left undone that we were supposed to do. God will make sure of that. I too can testify to the truth that serving God is indeed to live a life that is truly without regrets!

5) We need to serve God so as to be an example for others to follow!

If we have lived long enough, we have likely all heard the saying that none of us is an island unto ourselves. All of us impact the lives of others in ways that we are often not aware of. For instance, after God had called me as an evangelist, and just before I left family and friends to go to the place of service God was sending me to, the local church I had been attending had a cake and coffee time after the evening service the last Sunday I was with them. And after the time of refreshments, one of the elders, who was also a very close friend, gathered everyone in one large room and gave me a gift on behalf of the local church. Then he asked those gathered there if anyone had anything to say to me before I left. Then for the next twenty minutes or so, a few people related instances where I had helped them in some way. What some of those people related were things that I was not even aware of, or were events which I had even totally forgotten about. This caught me by surprise, but it also taught me a lesson that we indeed impact the lives of others without even realizing it sometimes. The same is true for all of us, no matter who we are.

Another more recent example here concerns a woman whose husband has been part of my senior's support group for the last eight years. And for much of that time we were meeting Tuesday, Thursday, and Sunday afternoons, with this woman often joining us for the tea and refreshment part of our gathering. So when this woman died of cancer on April 11th in 2014, I ended up crying at least 13 times in the months that followed. I do not remember crying so much over someone since my own mother died at a fairly young age in 1988 and also my wife in 1994. I had not realized until this woman was gone that I had truly loved her as a friend, and how much she had impacted my life with her kindness, gentleness, and generosity. And that woman likely was not even aware that she was impacting my life in this way. Actually, neither did I realize just how much until she was gone.

So when it comes to the matter of serving God, we can be sure that someone is observing our life, whether we are aware of it or not. Sometimes it is only when we get to Heaven that we will see the full extent of the impact our lives have had on others. In an earlier book, I related how suicide and divorce negatively impacts whole families and even subsequent generations. How critical then in these last days that we impact the lives of all those about us – family, friends, coworkers, and acquaintances, by serving God, and in the process being an example for others to follow. Our focus does not need to be on trying to serve God in order to be an example to others. We only need to have our focus on serving God and God Himself will use our service to encourage others to also serve Him! We can count on that.

And so, we too as believers are all called of God to serve Him so as to be an example for others to follow, noting what God also says at 1 Corinthians 10:11, "Now these things happened to them as an example, and they were written for our instruction, upon whom the ends of the ages have come," also at Philippians 3:17, "Brethren, join in following my example, and observe those who walk according to the pattern you have in us," and also at 1 Thessalonians 1:6,7, "[6] You also became imitators of us and of the Lord, having received the word in much tribulation with the joy of the Holy Spirit, [7] so that you became an example to all the believers in Macedonia and in Achaia." May God enable all of us by His grace and power to be an example for others to follow by serving God in these last days!

6) We need to serve God simply because He is worthy of our service!

As we bring this chapter to a close, we would be remiss if we did not mention the most important reason for serving God, which is that He is most worthy of our service! When we take our eyes off ourselves long enough to look at God, we see One Who is holy, righteous, almighty, sovereign, good, loving, merciful, gracious, humble, faithful, kind, patient, gentle, and so on and so on. And what needs to be grasped here is that God gives us that look of Himself in two principal ways. The first is to see Him through His Son by The Holy Spirit, for when we look at His Son in human flesh, The Lord Jesus Christ, in the gospel accounts of Matthew, Mark, Luke, and John, we then see what God is like, for The Son is the exact visible representation of what God, Who is invisible, is like (noting John 14:9; Colossians 1:15; Hebrews 1:3).

Then the second way God gives us a look at Himself is the way that He deals with us through His Son by The Holy Spirit from the moment that He gives us a spiritual birth into His family. Which one of us does not look at our mother as the woman who gave us birth into this world, carrying us in her womb for nine months, then in her arms for as many months again as she held us and nursed us at her breasts. As the primary caregiver, she showed us the extent of her love through her selfless service to us after we were born and while we lived at home.

It is not surprising then that God uses that truth about mothers to spur believers to act toward others in the same way, noting what we read at 1 Thessalonians 2:7,8, "[7] But we proved to be gentle among you, as a nursing mother tenderly cares for her own children. [8] Having so fond an affection for you, we were well-pleased to impart to you not only the gospel of God but also our own lives, because you had become very dear to us." Since this is the case with mothers, who are but created and finite human beings still having a sinful nature, think just how much better God deals with us and makes Himself known to us after He gives us a spiritual birth, as One Who is uncreated, eternal, and holy!

Therefore, the more we see God in His dealings with us as we grow spiritually as a child of God, then the more willing we will be to serve Him, for then we will be seeing Him as He is, as truly worthy of our service!

When we also pause and consider what the alternative to serving God is, which is to serve self, then there really is no comparison. Serving self may bring us momentary satisfaction to our pride, but no lasting satisfaction like serving God does. What we need to ever remember is that God designed us not only to be in fellowship with Him, when He created us in His image (noting Genesis 1:26), but God also designed us to derive our greatest satisfaction and contentment only when we are serving Him.

For what also needs to be grasped here is that God, as our Designer and Creator, knows what our deepest needs are, and He meets those needs as a BYPRODUCT of our serving Him! In other words, when we set out to serve God because He is worthy of our service, He meets our deepest needs, which only He fully understands and which only He can fully meet.

Let us note for instance what God says to us at Psalm 37:4, "Delight yourself in the Lord; and He will give you the desires of your heart. " When looking at this verse in my second book, titled, "Finding Comfort And Encouragement In The Promises Of God In The Last Days," it was there said that one was delighting in God when one was living by God's imparted life, which is His righteousness. And as we do so, God gives us the deepest desires of our hearts, because now we are at the place where God can meet our deepest needs, because we are not serving self, but rather are now serving Him. As we serve God, we find that at the same time He is serving us!

More than this, what we find is that just as we cannot outgive God, so too is it true that we cannot outserve Him either! For what also needs to be grasped here is that God is out to conform us to His image, which is the image of His Son. And which one of us can outserve and outgive God's precious Son? For while briefly here on earth sharing our humanity,

The Son served God His Father by only and always doing His will and then gave His life as ransom for the sins of mankind, that God would have a basis for forgiving us our sins! Therefore, let us, as those who have been given a spiritual birth into God's family, serve God willingly out of love for Him, for truly He is worthy of our service!

"Now to Him who is able to do far more abundantly beyond all that we ask or think…"

Ephesians 3:20 in part

"And my God will supply all your needs according to His riches in glory in Christ Jesus."

Philippians 4:19

CHAPTER SEVEN

God is more than able to meet our every need!

What we want to do in this chapter is to impress upon the hearts and minds of every person reading this book that God is more than able to meet one's every need! For what needs to be grasped here is that two of God's attributes are His ALMIGHTINESS, which speaks of His having UNLIMITED POWER to accomplish all He has set out to do in time, which includes fulfilling every promise that He has made in His word; and also His SOVEREIGNTY, which speaks of His FULL CONTROL over all persons, events, and circumstances that could possibly occur in God's creation in time! What this means then is that no matter what one's need might be, whether health, finances, finding employment, finding a spouse, healing a relationship, God is more than able to meet that need!

To encourage us further, let us note what God tells us in His word at Romans 8:28, where we read, "And we know that GOD CAUSES ALL THINGS TO WORK TOGETHER FOR GOOD to those who love God, to those who are called according to His purpose." If you have read this verse before and have wondered what God means by the "all things" here, then please be aware that God means what we might consider 'good' and also what we might consider as 'bad' or 'not so good.' For instance, we might consider finding one's soul mate a good thing, but one might not consider getting cancer to be a good thing. And so the "good" of the "all things" here is what we would consider as desirable. In other words, if we had a choice the 'good' of the "all things" is what we would choose for ourselves; while what we would not choose, although not evil, would not be the 'bad' or the 'not so good.'

However, what God is saying in this verse is that He takes all that occurs to us as believers in this life, whether we consider it 'good' or 'bad,' God takes all that and works in such a way that in the end of our life here on earth, we will see that God will indeed have caused all things to work together for our good, in terms of our being at that point more than satisfied with all God has done for us after salvation!

To reinforce this truth, let us note what God says four verses further on at Romans 8:32, where we read, "He who did not spare His own Son, but delivered Him over for us all, HOW WILL HE NOT ALSO WITH HIM FREELY GIVE US ALL THINGS?" The amazing truth to grasp here is that since God GAVE HIS ALL, WHEN HE GAVE US HIS SON, then can any one of us expect Him to give us any less in anything we might need while a child of His on earth after salvation? And of course, the answer, if one believes what God says at Romans 8:28, is 'no,' in that God is more than willing to give us "all things," which includes all that we need!

What is also instructive to notice here is that the "all things" at Romans 8:28 consists of both, what we would choose as desirable to happen to us and also what we would not choose as desirable to happen to us. However, the "all things" at Romans 8:32 consists of ONLY WHAT WE WOULD CONSIDER AS GOOD OR DESIRABLE TO HAPPEN TO US!

But what needs to be grasped in all this is that just as we do not reward our children for rebellion against us as parents, because we know that this would only encourage further rebellion, and would not be an act of love toward one's child; then the same applies with us as believers in our relationship with God. Only when we are walking with Him in the light of His word, serving Him on earth by carrying out His will, can God out of love for us, meet our every need!

"Trust in the Lord with all your heart and do not lean on your own understanding. In all your ways acknowledge Him, and He will make your paths straight."

Proverbs 3:5,6

CHAPTER EIGHT

A last word!

What is very important to grasp, as we bring this book to a close, is that we all need to place our lives in God's Hands and say to Him, no matter what occurs, "Your will be done, not my own will!" And this requires absolute trust in Him, which should not be hard if we remember how our salvation began. The moment we believed on God's Son, The Lord Jesus Christ – namely that He died for me, was buried to put my sins away from God's sight forever, was then resurrected from the dead the third day and brought to His Father's right Hand in Heaven again – we received the forgiveness of sins ever committed against God and started receiving God's eternal life to live by!

Did any one of us see The Holy Spirit come to indwell our human spirit? Did any see one's sins being removed? Did any see that eternal life enter us? Well, no. We simply believed based on the results that we experienced, such as realizing that our burden and guilt of sin was gone, and we had such peace and joy filling our hearts as God's life flooded our whole being. And suddenly we had new desires like we never had before, such as wanting to read God's word and suddenly calling God, "Father," which was something we never did before! And as we read God's word, we believed it and sought to align our lives in accordance with God's word, because our trust was in Him.

The reality is that we ALL start our Christian life with God after salvation as the man, who while on holidays on a remote island, started doing some exploring. And while following a path near the edge of a cliff, he was paying so much attention to the beauty out over the ocean that he came too close to the edge and was about to fall down the cliff when he quickly grabbed a clump of branches with one hand and hung on for dear life, as he dangled from what seemed to be at least a couple of hundred feet up. Scared to death at that point, he yelled out as loud as he could, “Is there anyone up there?” All of a sudden, he heard this voice clear as crystal say to him, LET GO.” At that, our dangling tourist looked down and quickly assessed his situation. He could see that there was some water below him, but he did not know if it was deep enough, or if there were rocks just below the surface. And so, in desperation he looked up and yelled out again, “Is there anyone else up there?” In a similar fashion, we too, even as children of God in salvation, often regard God as less than God, even though He is in reality The One with Whom nothing is impossible, except to sin!

So while the above fictional story might bring a smile to our face, we can be sure that from the moment we become a child of God in salvation, God has our lives completely planned out, even to the smallest detail. Actually, God knew us even in eternity past, before creation even took place! But the reality is that we start our lives as a child of God as we started our physical lives into this world, as babes, totally dependent on others, with those others being our parents at first. However, once we came to know God in salvation, those others that we now depended upon was God The Father working through His Son, The Lord Jesus Christ, by His Holy Spirit!

And so, like our exploring tourist in the fictional account above, we too are reluctant to ‘let go,’ not yet realizing that God is not only in total control of all events, circumstances, and persons that we ever have contact with while one earth, but also more than able to meet our every need! God knows, as our Loving and Caring Father, that we are but babes as yet, and that we need to grow up in the faith, which takes time. God also knows, especially if we are much older when coming to personally know Him in salvation, that we have been living many years without ever giving Him a second thought, with our only concern in many cases being but 'me, myself, and I.' Everything we did, said, and thought was to a large measure done, said, and thought for the benefit of our constant companion: Self!

That thankfully changes as we grow toward spiritual maturity, so that the longer we have been a child of God, the more we have learned to trust God wholly. For then we start to ponder the road that we have been on for many years after salvation and start to see that God has been there all along, providing, protecting, teaching, correcting, disciplining; and always with loving care. We start to learn what real love is, which is a total giving of oneself for another, and then realize that this is indeed what God did when He gave His Son (John 3:16) and this is also what His Son did when He gave Himself for us (1 John 3:16). The end result is that we want to spend the rest of our lives here no longer living for self, but rather only for the will of God, with our greatest delight being to bring honor and glory to Him!

So what we need to realize in closing is that we started our new life with God BY FAITH, that is, BY SIMPLY TRUSTING HIM, which was shown by living our lives in accordance with His word! This, dear readers, is what we need to continue to do day by day, whether we have been saved one day or fifty years; whether there is normalcy in the world or not, for what is truly important is living to please God, by living in accordance with His word, thereby carrying out His will for our lives, which is the purpose for which He saved us! Once we are there, then we will have found THE TRUE AND ONLY NORMAL THAT REALLY MATTERS!

To God alone be all praise, honor, and glory, with thanksgiving, both now and forevermore! Amen, amen, and amen.

ADDENDUM A

The nature of man and the consequence of sin!

What we would like to do in this Addendum is to provide readers with what God says about the nature of man as originally created by God, and what we all became as a result of the sin of Adam and Eve. And so, the first basic truth to be aware of here is that the first man created by God, whom God called "Adam," and the woman that God then created to be his wife, and who was named "Eve," were literal people, and are the original couple from whom the whole human race comes from.

What is also important to remember is that Adam and Eve were not only actual people, but were also representative of the whole human race, meaning that any other man or woman in existence after them would have done the very same as they did, had they been in their place, and would not have acted any differently. In other words, God created us all with a like nature, so that what one does under a certain set of circumstances, then all will likewise do under the same set of circumstances, due to the initial makeup of our human nature by God. And so we are to see that all mankind has the same composition and nature, in that each human being comes from the same man and woman God first created.

Then the second basic truth we need to be aware of here is what the constituent parts of man were, as first created by God, noting here what we are told at Genesis 2:7, when God first created Adam, where we read, "Then the Lord God formed man of dust from the ground, and breathed into his nostrils the breath of life; and man became a living being." What we are to see from this verse of the Bible is that the constituent parts of man consist of a body, "formed... of dust" by God, into which God "breathed into his nostrils the breath of life," which is the human spirit, so that man "became a living being," that is, a living soul. And these then are the three constituent parts of man that God speaks about in His word, as we see Him confirm for us at 1 Thessalonians 5:23, where we read, "Now may the God of peace Himself sanctify you entirely; and may your spirit and soul and body be preserved complete, without blame at the coming of our Lord Jesus Christ."

What is then important to know is that God gave the human spirit for man to be able to commune with God, Who is revealed in the Bible as being a spirit Being, noting what we read at John 4:24, "God is spirit, and those who worship Him must worship in spirit and truth." This is how Adam was communing with God before he sinned, through his spirit, or we could say 'spiritually.' At that point, there was as yet no sin in Adam to prevent his communing with God by his spirit, that is, spiritually. Although, all of that would change the moment Adam sinned against God.

We are then to see that the "soul" is the human part of man, being the component of our being which renders us a person, and which God gave man so as to be able to commune with other human beings. It is the soul of man that contains our will, our mind, our emotions, our heart (as the inner part of the soul), and our conscience. There is also a heart of the body, which is the organ which pumps our blood to keep us alive physically. In contrast to this, the heart of the soul is the inner part of the soul of man, while the human spirit is the inner part of the whole man.

And what is important to remember about the spirit, soul, and body at this point is that the spirit and soul are immaterial and unseen, while the body, is the only part of us that is material and can be seen, being the shell that holds the spirit and soul of man. Once created by God in the first man, Adam, and then passed on through childbirth, the spirit and the soul, which never dies, go on for eternity! Only the human body ages and dies!

Now we are to see that there came a day when God tested Adam, when He said to him in the garden of Eden, which was here on earth, what we now read at Genesis 2:16,17, "[16] The Lord God commanded the man, saying, "From any tree of the garden you may eat freely; [17] but from the tree of the knowledge of good and evil you shall not eat, for in the day that you eat from it you will surely die."

Unfortunately, there also came a day when Adam lost the state of innocence, which is the moment Adam disobeyed God's command above and did partake of the forbidden tree, noting now what we read at Genesis 3:1-6, "[1] Now the serpent was more crafty than any beast of the field which the Lord God had made. And he said to the woman, "Indeed, has God said, 'You shall not eat from any tree of the garden'?" [2] The woman said to the serpent, "From the fruit of the trees of the garden we may eat; [3] but from the fruit of the tree which is in the middle of the garden, God has said, 'You shall not eat from it or touch it, or you will die.' "[4] The serpent said to the woman, "You surely will not die! [5] For God knows that in the day you eat from it your eyes will be opened, and you will be like God, knowing good and evil." [6] When the woman saw that the tree was good for food, and that it was a delight to the eyes, and that the tree was desirable to make one wise, she took from its fruit and ate; and she gave also to her husband with her, and he ate."

The moment that Adam ate of that forbidden tree in the garden of Eden, he became not only a sinner by practice, but also a sinner by nature, in that all which came from Adam from that moment onward would be sin in God's sight, that is, all thoughts, actions, and words. And that is why, dear reader, that God needed to send His eternal and sinless Son from Heaven to earth to take on a body like we have, but in the innocence of Adam, and then after thirty-three years of life here on earth of living only by the righteousness of God, as a Pattern for us, He died in our place at the cross, for the penalty for sin, as we saw at Genesis 2:17, is death.

When one comes to believe in God through faith in His Son, The Lord Jesus Christ – namely that He died for our sins, was buried, and was raised again the third day – then one receives from God the forgiveness of sins (which includes every single sin committed from the age of accountability onward) and eternal life with Him. That eternal life is to be seen as God's own righteous life, or righteousness, so that when a believer lives by God's righteousness, then all one thinks, does, and says is right in God's sight.

Therefore, how important that the child of God see that from the moment of salvation onward, the child of God is no longer to live by one's self life, which is drawing life from the soul, which is now sinful by nature, as we have seen above, but rather the child of God is to live by God's righteousness alone. This is why this truth is stated so emphatically, simply because one cannot be pleasing to God unless one is living by God's righteousness, that is, by His own life being imparted, which is eternal life!

Then the last truth which is important to be aware of here as a believer is that the sin of Adam and Eve had a consequence for the whole human race. And at this point, we need to mention again the fact that Adam was not only a literal human being, but Adam was also a representative man, in that through him, and what happens to him here, God then uses this to teach the whole of the human race about certain concepts, such as sin and death. For instance, in the New Testament, God says at Romans 5:12, "Therefore, just as through one man (Adam) sin entered into the world, and death through (Adam's) sin, and so death spread to all men, because all sinned (that is, all personally do so at the age of accountability)…"

This is a very important verse, for here we learn that through Adam, as our representative man, who not only became a sinner by practice, but also a sinner by nature, and since we are all descendants of this one man, then all human beings incur at birth Adam's sinful nature, so that shortly after reaching the age of accountability – which is the age at which a child first learns right from wrong, and chooses the wrong, thereby becoming personally accountable to God for one's sin against Him – when one also sins against God, one not only becomes a sinner by practice, but also a sinner by nature.

All human beings can identify with the truth just stated. I know that when I was a child my parents did not have to teach me how to sin, that came naturally! In fact, my parents constantly had to show me the right way; for of my own, I kept going astray from what was right. That is because I had reached the age of accountability and now had a sinful nature that only ever wanted to sin.

If you are a parent, you have probably painfully noticed already that this is also true in your own children. There is nothing unusual happening here, we are only experiencing the consequence of Adam's sin, a sin, we must ever remember, that any of us would have also committed had we been in Adam's place, since he was but representative of us all. Therefore, as a consequence of Adams's sin, the whole human race not only became sinners by practice, but also sinners by nature!

"Jesus said to him, "I am the way, and the truth, and the life; no one comes to the Father but through Me."
"

John 14:6

ADDENDUM B

/ For those who may not as yet know God

Possibly you have been reading this book and have become aware of not knowing this God Who created us and gave us physical life into this world, and up to now has allowed you to live on earth. However, you do have the desire to know God in a personal way. If this is the case, then this Addendum has been written specifically for you.

And what God wants you to have in coming to know Him is the peace and joy which comes in knowing that all of your sins committed in your lifetime are forgiven and that you have eternal life with God. And so, your greatest need at the moment is to make peace with God so as to go to Heaven, which is God's eternal home. And so, this Addendum will help to bring that about by pointing you to God so as to come to faith in Him.

And as we begin, we need to note a most important promise which God makes at Romans 6:23 to all those who do not yet know Him, "For the wages of sin is death, but the free gift of God is eternal life in Christ Jesus our Lord." The good news here is that God offers you eternal life with Him as a free gift, which is to be obtained in His Son, Jesus Christ. What God does not do in this verse from the Bible is tell us 'how' to obtain that eternal life with Him.

Another verse which we can look at where God does let us know 'how' one can obtain that eternal life with Him is noting what God tells us at John 3:16, "For God so loved the world, that He gave His only begotten Son, that whoever believes in Him shall not perish, but have eternal life." Now the added truth which God makes known here is that the eternal life, which He gives to a human being as a free gift, is for those who believe in His Son.

Then the question is: What is it that I am to believe about God's Son, Jesus Christ, which will lead God to give me eternal life with Him forever? And the beauty of God is that He never leaves us guessing, especially when it comes to having a personal relationship with Him, which He desires us to have. Therefore, we should not be surprised when God gives us the answer to our question in what He tells us at 1 Corinthians 15:1-4, "[1] Now I make known to you, brethren, the gospel which I preached to you, which also you received, in which also you stand, [2] by which also you are saved, if you hold fast the word which I preached to you, unless you believed in vain. [3] For I delivered to you as of first importance what I also received, that Christ died for our sins according to the Scriptures, [4] and that He was buried, and that He was raised on the third day according to the Scriptures..."

Therefore, "the gospel," which simply means 'good news,' which God wants you to hear and believe in order to "be saved," which simply refers to you coming to know God and have eternal life with Him, is that His Son has already died for you, has already been buried, and has already been raised from the dead again the third day after His death, in order that God would have a basis by which to forgive you of all your sins, which are all against Him, and to freely give you eternal life with Him, for simply believing this message in your heart.

One thing which often prevents a person from believing the gospel at this point is not seeing oneself as a sinner before a Holy God. When we look at ourselves by our own assessment, and especially when we compare ourselves with others around us, we often think of ourselves as being better than others, and so good enough to enter Heaven in our present condition. The problem with this is that it is the product of our own thinking and is not God's assessment of our situation.

God's assessment of our situation is as He tells us at Romans 3:10-12,23 in part, "[10] as it is written, "There is none righteous, not even one... [11] there is none who seeks for God [12] all have turned aside... there is none who does good, there is not even one... [23] for all have sinned and fall short of the glory of God..." Quite a different assessment of the human race from that which we as human beings often have of ourselves, is this not? But why would God have such an assessment of the whole human race? For the answer to that question, we need to be aware that God is Creator of all that exists, so that when God created the first man, Adam, at the beginning of time, God created him in innocence, meaning that Adam as first created by God neither knew good nor evil, nor was there any sin anywhere in God's original sinless creation.

However, the day came when God tested Adam with a command, saying to him in the garden of Eden here on earth, which was the perfect environment which God had for him, what we now read at Genesis 2:16,17, "[16] The Lord God commanded the man, saying, "From any tree of the garden you may eat freely; [17] but from the tree of the knowledge of good and evil you shall not eat, for in the day that you eat from it you will surely die." How important to see here that God gave Adam, who although a real person was also representative of the whole human race, the warning of the penalty of death for disobedience to His command.

Unfortunately, the day did come when Adam did partake of the forbidden tree and thereby did sin against God. The moment that happened, Adam not only became a sinner by practice, but also a sinner by nature. One thing my parents had to continually do while under their care was to restrain me from continually going the wrong way, for it seemed that of myself I could not do good, but kept going into sin. The reason this was happening is that from the age of accountability onwards, I had not only become a sinner by practice, but also a sinner by nature.

And here the age of accountability needs to be seen as being when as a young child in innocence - which moment is known only by God - one comes to learn the right from the wrong and chooses the wrong, thereby becoming personally accountable to God for one's own sin against Him, since all sin is first of all against Him. And that is why God can say at Romans 3:23 above that “all have sinned and fall short of the glory of God,” because God knows that all human beings will go the way of Adam, our representative man, which is also why God can say what He does in regards to the whole of the human race at Romans 5:12, where we read, ”Therefore, just as through one man (Adam) sin entered into the world, and death through sin, and so death spread to all men, because all sinned” (from the age of accountability onward). And so, we see that the whole human race is declared by God to not only be sinners by practice and by nature from the age of accountability onwards, but the whole of the human race is now subject to death! In other words, in God's sight the whole of the human race is under the judgment of the penalty of death, due to all being sinners by practice and by nature.

You will recall above, in the first verse we quoted from Romans 6:23, God did say there that “the wages of sin are death.” And what God means by “death” here is not just loss of physical life, when the physical body we have dies, but also has spiritual death in mind, which is far worse! Spiritual death has its beginning when a separation takes place between a person and God at the moment one becomes a sinner at the age of accountability and ends after the final judgment of time, when God forever casts away from His Presence those who before physical death refused to believe in His Son, The Lord Jesus Christ, thereby personally forfeiting the forgiveness of their sins and eternal life with God. And now all such will pay the penalty for their own sins in hell, away from the Presence of God forever.

It is in the midst of such a hopeless situation in which the whole of the human race found itself in that God TOOK THE INITIATIVE and sent His own eternally existing Son into the world, as born of a virgin in the innocence of Adam – so as not to inherit the sinful nature passed on from generation after generation from Adam onwards through the conception of the female – so that He might be the acceptable sacrifice offered to God His Father at the cross, there bearing our sins in His body, and there dying the death due our sins! God's Son, Jesus Christ, was then buried and raised from the dead the third day, to ever be alive, for it is through Him, on the basis of what God has done for us through His Son, that God The Father forgives our sins and imparts us eternal life.

Now, by God's grace and His enablement, may you see your need of God's Son to be Your Savior from the penalty due sin, which is death, not only physical, but also spiritual. And by God's grace, may He lead you to believe in His Son, Jesus Christ, and in believing, to receive the forgiveness of your sins and eternal life with Him forever! And based on the truth just shared, the author would now like to ask you a few questions, with the answer being just between yourself and God:

When God says at Romans 3:23, "for all have sinned and fall short of the glory of God," does that include you?

When God says at Romans 5:8, "But God demonstrates His own love toward us, in that while we were yet sinners, Christ died for us," were you included in Christ's death on behalf of sinners?

And when God further says at 1 Peter 3:18 in part, "For Christ also died for sins once for all, the just for the unjust, so that He might bring us to God, having been put to death in the flesh, but made alive in the spirit," were you part of the unjust for whom Christ died?

When God says at Romans 6:23, "For the wages of sin is death, but the free gift of God is eternal life in Christ Jesus our Lord," do you want that eternal life as a free gift from God?

When God says at John 3:16, “For God so loved the world, that He gave His only begotten Son, that whoever believes in Him shall not perish, but have eternal life,” do you now believe that Jesus Christ is indeed God’s Son in human flesh, Who came from Heaven to this earth to die in your place, so as to save you from ever experiencing the judgment of God leading to an eternal separation from God in hell?

And when God then further says to you at Isaiah 55:6, “Seek the Lord while He may be found; call upon Him while He is near,” for His further promise to you here is as we read at Romans 10:9-11,13, “[9] that if you confess with your mouth Jesus as Lord, and believe in your heart that God raised Him from the dead, you will be saved (that is, you will now enter into a personal relationship with God by faith); [10] for with the heart a person believes, resulting in righteousness (that is, in now receiving God’s own righteous and eternal life to live by), and with the mouth he confesses, resulting in salvation (that is, in now receiving as a free gift the forgiveness of sins and eternal life with God). [11] For the Scripture says, “Whoever believes in Him will not be disappointed...” [13] for “Whoever will call on the name of the Lord will be saved.” Will you now call upon God from your heart in your own words being mindful of your answer to each question that have just been asked?

The author’s prayer for you at this point, as you now call upon God by His grace, is what we read at Romans 15:13, “Now may the God of hope fill you with all joy and peace in believing, so that you will abound in hope by the power of the Holy Spirit.”

/ The next book

As this book is being published, God has given His servant the go-ahead to write another book, titled "God's First Letter To The Corinthians." In case it is not the next book, the reader may want to check with the author's website to see what book has been published:

http://www.pilgrimpathwaypublications.com

If you have found this book profitable, or any other of the author's books, please feel free to let family, friends, and co-workers know about this book and the other books. The author is not on any social media sites, so he relies on God and readers to spread the word. May God bless you for doing so!

www.ingramcontent.com/pod-product-compliance
Lightning Source LLC
LaVergne TN
LVHW090124160826
845673LV00015B/834

9798351782003